First paperback edition published 1992
by Barron's Educational Series, Inc.

First English language edition published 1982
by Barron's Educational Series, Inc.

All inquiries should be addressed to:
Barron's Educational Series, Inc.
250 Wireless Boulevard
Hauppauge, NY 11788

International Standard Book No. 0-8120-5464-4 (hardcover)
0-8120-1452-9 (paperback)

Library of Congress Catalog Card No. 82-11563

Library of Congress Cataloging-in-Publication Data

Lepscky, Ibi.
   Albert Einstein / Ibi Lepscky; illustrated by
Paolo Cardoni; translated by Ruth Parlé Craig.
— 1st English language ed.

   22 p.: col. ill.; 26 cm.

   Summary: A biography of the great scientist,
for very young readers, focusing on his boyhood
during which he seemed so different from other
children.
   ISBN 0-8120-5464-4 (hardcover)
        0-8120-1452-9 (paperback)

   1. Einstein, Albert, 1879–1955—Juvenile
literature. 2. Physicists—Biography—Juvenile
literature. ₁1. Einstein, Albert, 1879–1955. 2.
Physicists₁ I. Cardoni, Paolo, ill. II. Title.

QC16.E5L38 1982   530'.092'4—dc19   82-11563
                  ₁B₁ ₁92₁   AACR 2 MARC

                                                AC

PRINTED IN HONG KONG
345 9927 98765432 (Paperback) (Hardcover) 2345 9927 98765

Ibi Lepscky

Albert Einstein

Illustrated by Paolo Cardoni
Translated by Ruth Parlé Craig

BARRON'S

About one hundred years ago, there lived a boy named
Albert Einstein.
     Albert was a strange boy.
     Always absentminded.
     Always messy.
     It was a difficult job for him to tie his shoes.

But he knew how to play the violin very well.

He did not like to play marbles or ball like other boys his age. Instead, he enjoyed looking for hours and hours at the shape of a leaf and playing with wooden blocks like a little child.

He disliked long sleeves, and as soon as he could, *snip* went the scissors as he cut his sleeves above the elbow.

He was not interested in the boys in his neighborhood, who invited him to play war. He preferred to chase the white chickens scratching in the garden and to try to make friends with them.

Albert felt happy only in the company of his little
sister, Maja, whom he loved very much and who looked
exactly like him. They were as alike as two drops of water.

"Albert is stupid," said his cousins when they came for a visit and tried to make him join in their games.

Albert ignored them and, with his sister, watched a colony of ants busy at work. He was a child different from others.

His parents loved him very much, but they were very worried about him.

"Albert is a good boy," said his father one night. "But I would like it if he would study a little more and if he would show some interest in history and geography."

It was true. Albert did not like school. He hated history and geography, and he refused to memorize any lessons. He was interested only in learning arithmetic.

"It would be nice if you could leave, Albert," a teacher told him one day. "Your behavior at school, so distracted and absentminded, and your poor interest in all I teach set bad examples for the whole class."

Albert did not even like sports and gymnastics. His classmates gave him the nickname of "Albert the Incapable."

One day, an older boy dared him by saying, "Look in my eyes if you are brave enough."

Albert did not even realize it was a dare—he was so unaware of things. With his arms hanging at his sides and a faraway look on his face, he seemed lost in another world. And he gently replied, "Excuse me, but I'm not interested in your eyes."

The older boy was confused and left, grumbling to himself.

That night, watching Albert outside, his father spoke to his mother. "I don't understand how a child could spend so many hours looking at the sky."

His mother smiled and said, "He is trying to see God. He imagines that God is hidden among the clouds, comfortably stretched out in an armchair of granite."

"Oh," sighed his father. "Who will ever be able to understand what Albert has in his mind?"

Albert's mother felt a special love and tenderness for Albert. She painted his picture on a little cup, and for the occasion, he was unusually well-groomed. The little cup was always displayed on the family's fireplace.

Albert's mother loved music very much, and in the
evenings, she and Albert would improvise little concerts for
the rest of the family. She would be at the piano and Albert
at the violin.

One day, when Albert had a fever and had to stay in bed for a few days, his father gave him a compass.

"Albert, you can pretend to be the captain of a ship," said his father, "and control the route with the compass."

But Albert was not interested in the game his father suggested. He wanted to know right away why the compass needle was pointing to the big *N* and what were magnetic fields all about and where were the poles of the earth. He asked question after question. It seemed they would never end.

Finally his father, exhausted, said curtly, "Because that's the way it is. That's all."

Later, Albert's father, thinking back about the boy's questions, was amazed that they were such thoughtful questions, so precise and sharp. Suddenly, he realized the truth about Albert. It was a truth that filled him with anguish, pride, and tenderness.

Albert was indeed a child different from all others. His gaze, which everyone thought to be absentminded, really reflected a very busy mind, a mind that was exploring places where nobody else could follow. It was the mind of a genius.

Albert's father was not mistaken.

When Albert grew up, his interest in every process of nature and science never stopped. He became a great scientist and developed new theories in physics that radically changed people's ideas about the universe. He discovered scientific truths never known before.

His mind made some of the greatest contributions in the history of human thought.